CALCULATOR PRACTICE

The four rules, investigations, codes and patterns

Alan Brighouse, David Godber, Peter Patilla

**A Piccolo Original
Piccolo Books**

A note to parents

This book has been designed to complement and reinforce much of the mathematics taught at school, but using a more informal approach. The calculator activities have been selected to increase and enrich the child's mathematical ability, as well as to give confidence in using a calculator. The main aims of the book are to:

develop mathematical thinking
explore number patterns
encourage and improve the ability to estimate
reinforce known concepts
develop new concepts

Calculators allow these areas to be developed.

Calculator Practice encourages children to work at their own pace. Occasionally they may call for help. When this happens, don't give your child the answer, but attempt by your questions to encourage the child to find the solution for herself. Give plenty of praise. The pages of the book can be done in any order. Some pages may be slightly more difficult than others so do not let the child become bogged down in an activity.

It is important that the work is taken in small stages. The activities are there to be enjoyed. When they stop being fun, it is time for a rest and a change. Therefore encourage the child to work in short bursts. Don't keep her at it until it becomes a chore.

Your involvement and interest is of the greatest importance, and although the activities can be tackled by the child alone, we hope the books will provide opportunities for discussion between you.

1. Butterflies

If there is a 7 in the answer, the children catch the butterfly.
Colour the butterflies they catch.

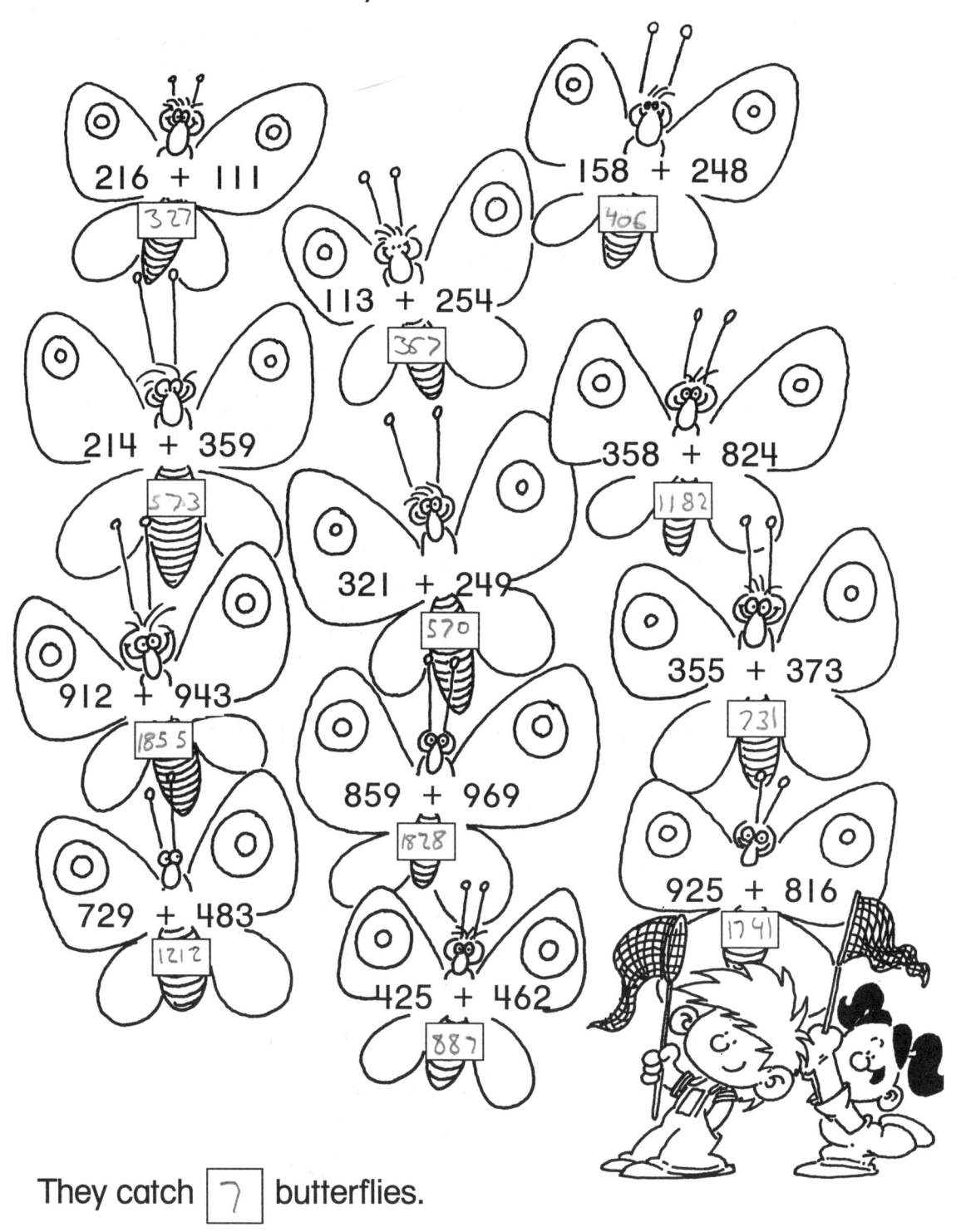

216 + 111
327

158 + 248
406

113 + 254
367

214 + 359
573

358 + 824
1182

321 + 249
570

912 + 943
1855

355 + 373
731

859 + 969
1828

729 + 483
1212

925 + 816
1741

425 + 462
887

They catch ⬚7⬚ butterflies.

2. Target

Use only the numbers 3 and 5, and the signs + and −. Fill the arrows like the one above, to make these targets.

Now use only 2 and 7, and + and −. Make these targets.

3. Four in a line

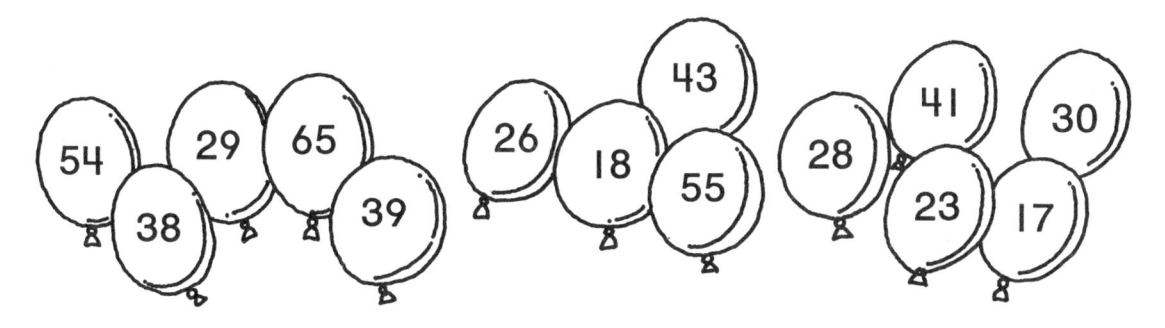

Balloons: 54, 29, 65, 38, 39, 26, 43, 18, 55, 28, 41, 30, 23, 17

You need ten counters. (Pieces of paper or buttons will do.)
Choose any two numbers from the balloons.
Add them together with your calculator.
If you can find the total on the grid, cover it with a counter.
Can you get four counters in a straight line?

If you use up all the counters start again.

80	73	51	83	64	84
95	47	91	69	61	57
71	53	62	59	99	82
98	58	66	35	67	48
72	55	81	94	40	68
93	56	44	88	52	85

5

4. Number magic

Write a number.
Add 25 to it.
Multiply by 2.
Subtract 4.
Divide by 2.
Subtract your first number.

4	8	1	3
	4	8	3	8
	9	6	7	6
	9	6	7	2
4	8	3	6
		2	3

Now you try starting with some different numbers. Follow the same instructions each time.

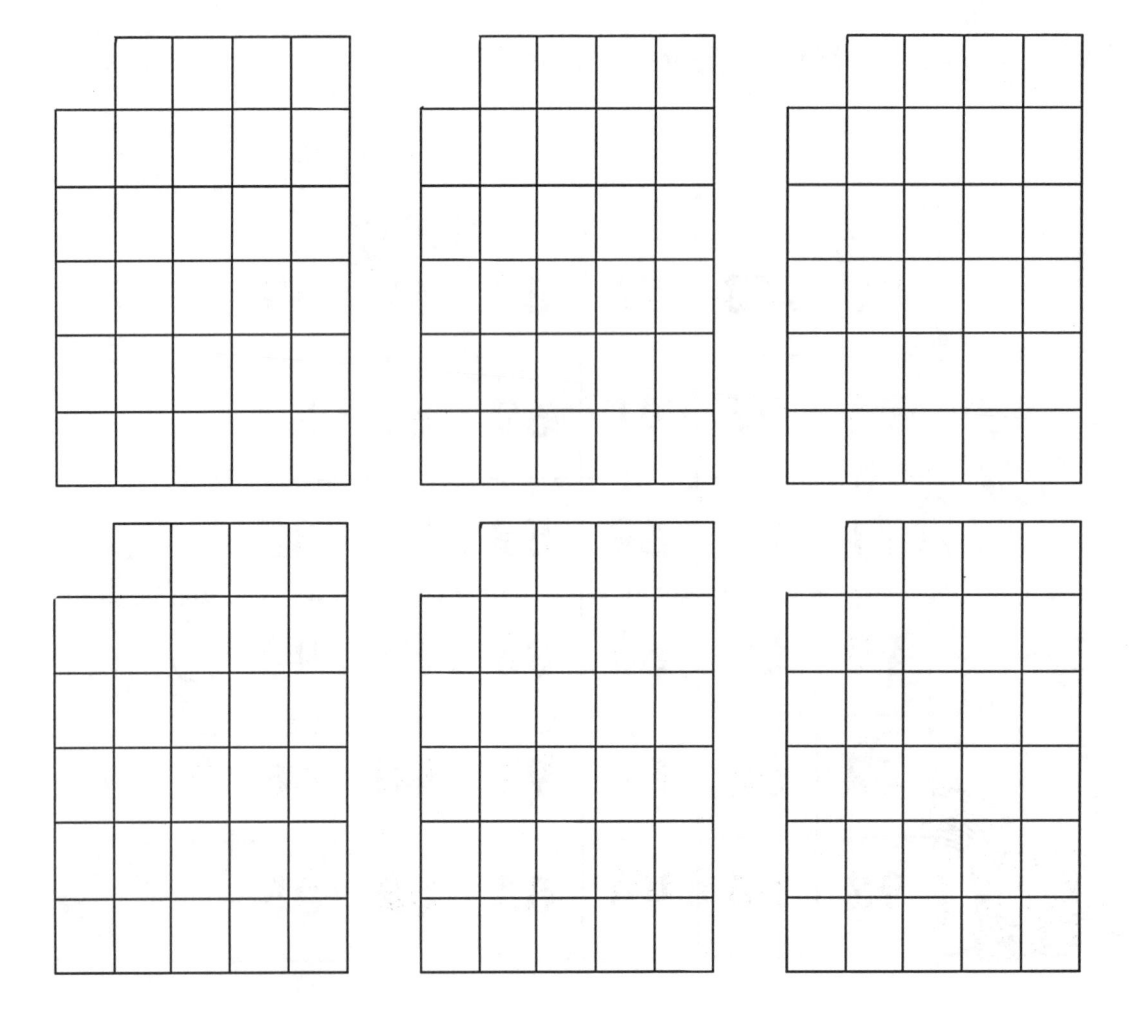

5. Just Two

You can use only the keys shown.
Can you make all the numbers 1 to 10?

1 [6][-][5][ ][ ][ ][=][ ]
2
3
4
5
6
7
8
9
10

6. Bats in the Belfry

If the answer is an even number, colour the bats.
How many have you coloured?

395 + 487

942 + 628

759 − 541

472 + 327

824 − 408

898 + 759

847 − 699

947 − 718

854 + 298

There are ☐ bats with an EVEN number in the answer.

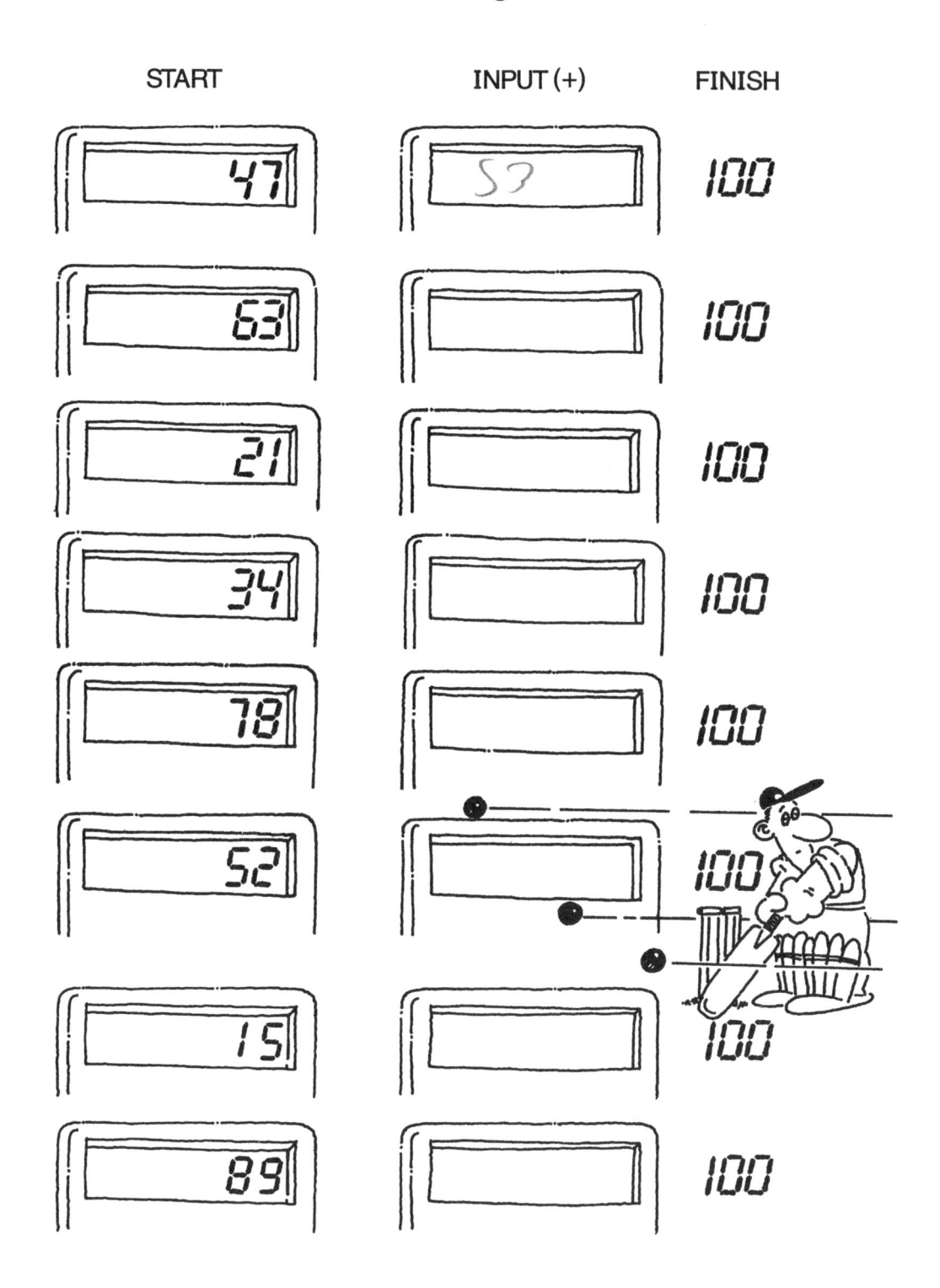

7. Making Centuries

With one input, change each starting number into a hundred.

START	INPUT (+)	FINISH
47	53	100
63		100
21		100
34		100
78		100
52		100
15		100
89		100

8. Taking Centuries

With one input, change each hundred into the answer shown.

START	INPUT (−)	FINISH
100		78
100		49
100		17
100		32
100		41
100		63
100		55
100		26

9. Find the Shape

Look at the two numbers in each square.
Find the difference between them.
If the difference is between 10 and 20 colour the square in.

You subtract the numbers to find the difference.

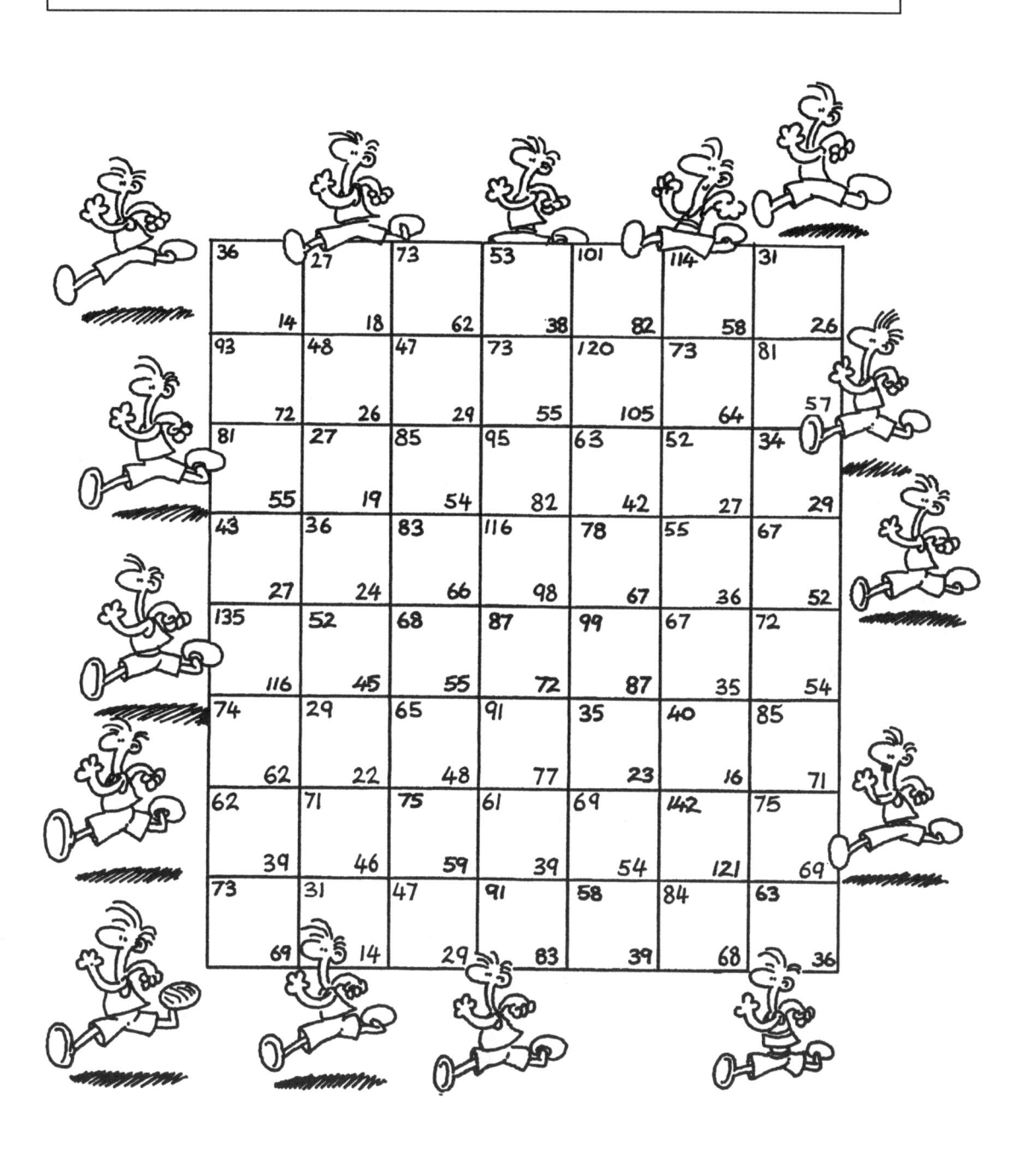

36	27	73	53	101	114	31
14	18	62	38	82	58	26
93	48	47	73	120	73	81
72	26	29	55	105	64	57
81	27	85	95	63	52	34
55	19	54	82	42	27	29
43	36	83	116	78	55	67
27	24	66	98	67	36	52
135	52	68	87	99	67	72
116	45	55	72	87	35	54
74	29	65	91	35	40	85
62	22	48	77	23	16	71
62	71	75	61	69	142	75
39	46	59	39	54	121	69
73	31	47	91	58	84	63
69	14	29	83	39	68	36

11

10. Wheel Code

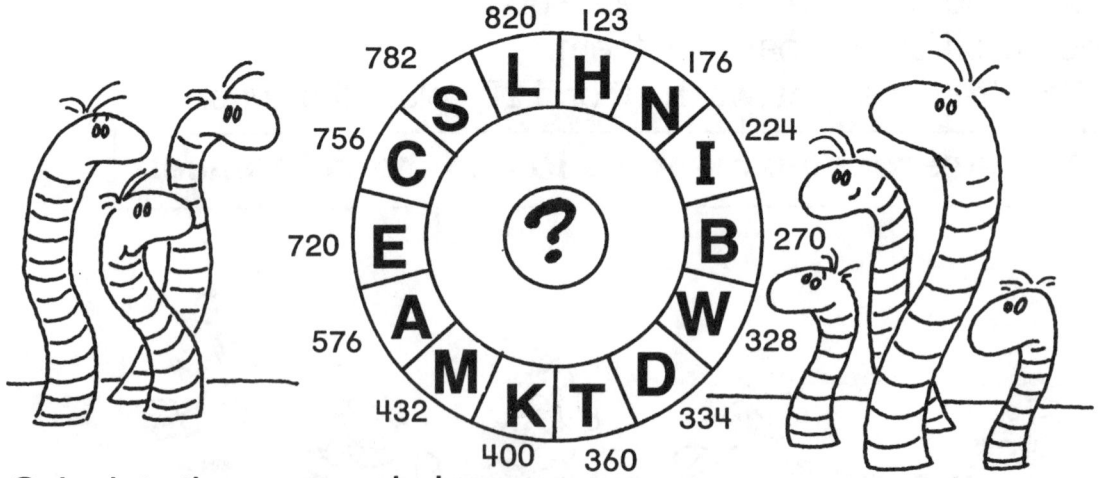

Wheel numbers/letters:
- 820 L
- 123 H
- 782 (S)
- 176 N
- 756 C
- 224 I
- 720 E
- 270 B
- 576 A
- 328 W
- 432 M
- 334 D
- 400 K
- 360 T

Calculate the answers below.
Find the answers in the wheel.
Write the letter which is by the answer.
The letters will spell what is in the mystery box.

24 × 24

456 + 326
144 + 288
319 + 257
431 + 389
529 + 291

18 × 15
41 × 20
36 × 16
42 × 18
25 × 16

824 − 248
764 − 588
512 − 178

984 ÷ 3
861 ÷ 7
896 ÷ 4
720 ÷ 2
720 ÷ 1

20 × 20
16 × 14
12 × 30
20 × 18
15 × 48
11 × 16

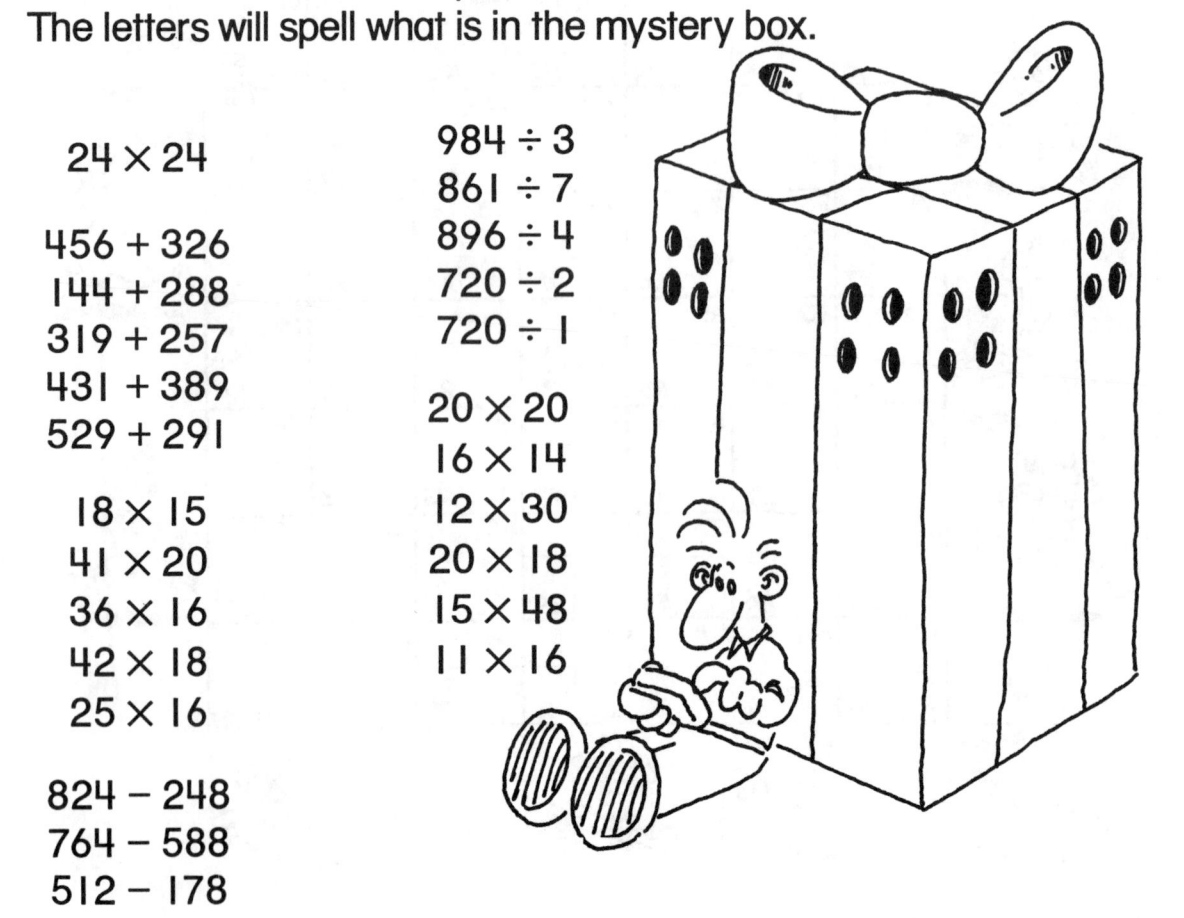

12

11. Count Down

USE   LIKE THIS   MAKE

| 3 8 9 | 9 ÷ 3 + 8 | (11) |

You must use all the three numbers shown.
Use + − × or ÷

USE   MAKE

7 8 9	☐ ☐ ☐	(10)
3 5 6	☐ ☐ ☐	(9)
3 4 6	☐ ☐ ☐	(8)
4 5 8	☐ ☐ ☐	(7)
2 7 8	☐ ☐ ☐	(6)
2 3 9	☐ ☐ ☐	(5)
3 6 8	☐ ☐ ☐	(4)
3 4 5	☐ ☐ ☐	(3)
6 7 8	☐ ☐ ☐	(2)
2 2 6	☐ ☐ ☐	(1)
9 3 3	☐ ☐ ☐	(0)

LIFT OFF

12. Number Words on Display

Put 57735 on your calculator display.
Turn the display upside down.
Write the word it spells.
Clue: It is what a shopkeeper does.

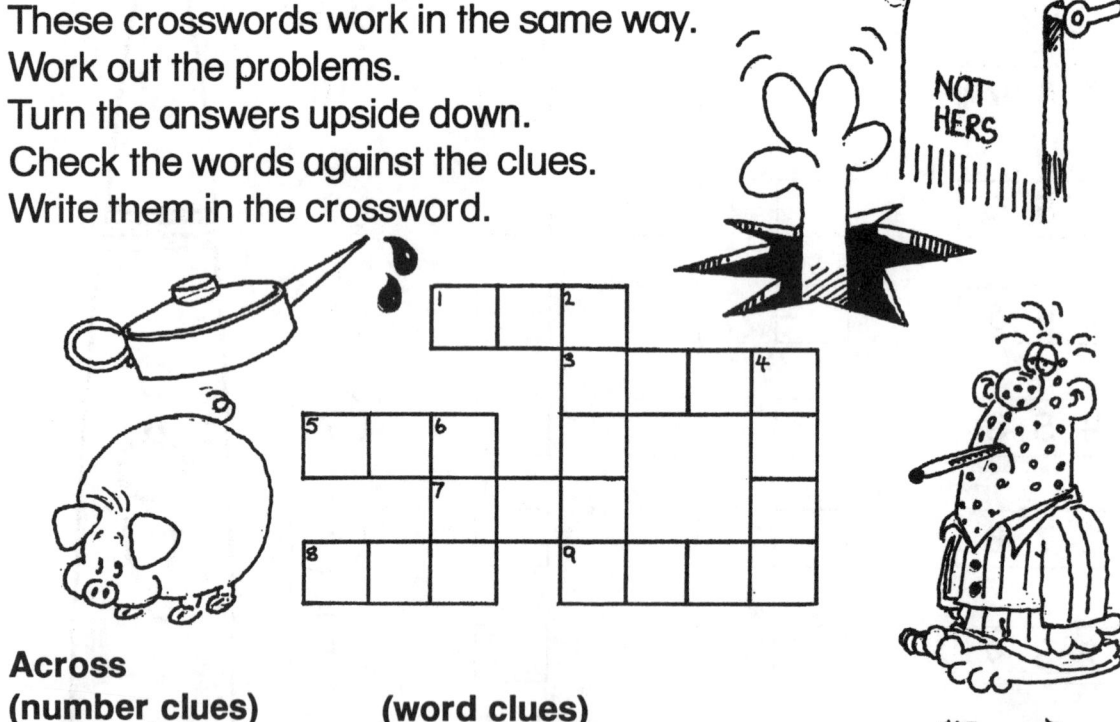

These crosswords work in the same way.
Work out the problems.
Turn the answers upside down.
Check the words against the clues.
Write them in the crossword.

Across
(number clues)   (word clues)
1 202 + 312   It belongs to him.
3 926 × 4   Buttons go through one.
5 900 − 129   Not well.
7 71 × 10   Thick greasy liquid.
8 299 + 305   Another name for a pig.
9 1879 × 3   These help us to walk and run.

Down
2 15469 × 5   Found on the sea shore.
4 3999 + 1664   Hens lay these.
6 1214 ÷ 2   Sit on it or burn it.

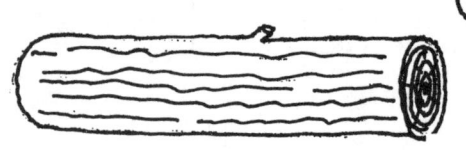

13. Zap the Digit

A digit is ZAPPED when it is changed to 0.
This is how to ZAP 138 with 3 inputs.

138	enter − 8	130	the 8 is zapped
130	enter − 30	100	the 3 is zapped
100	enter − 100	0	the 1 is zapped

Write the entry to ZAP these digits.

185 Zap 8 ____ Zap 1 ____ Zap 5 ____

239 Zap 2 ____ Zap 3 ____ Zap 9 ____

472 Zap 2 ____ Zap 4 ____ Zap 7 ____

574 Zap 4 ____ Zap 7 ____ Zap 5 ____

816 Zap 8 ____ Zap 6 ____ Zap 1 ____

391 Zap 1 ____ Zap 3 ____ Zap 9 ____

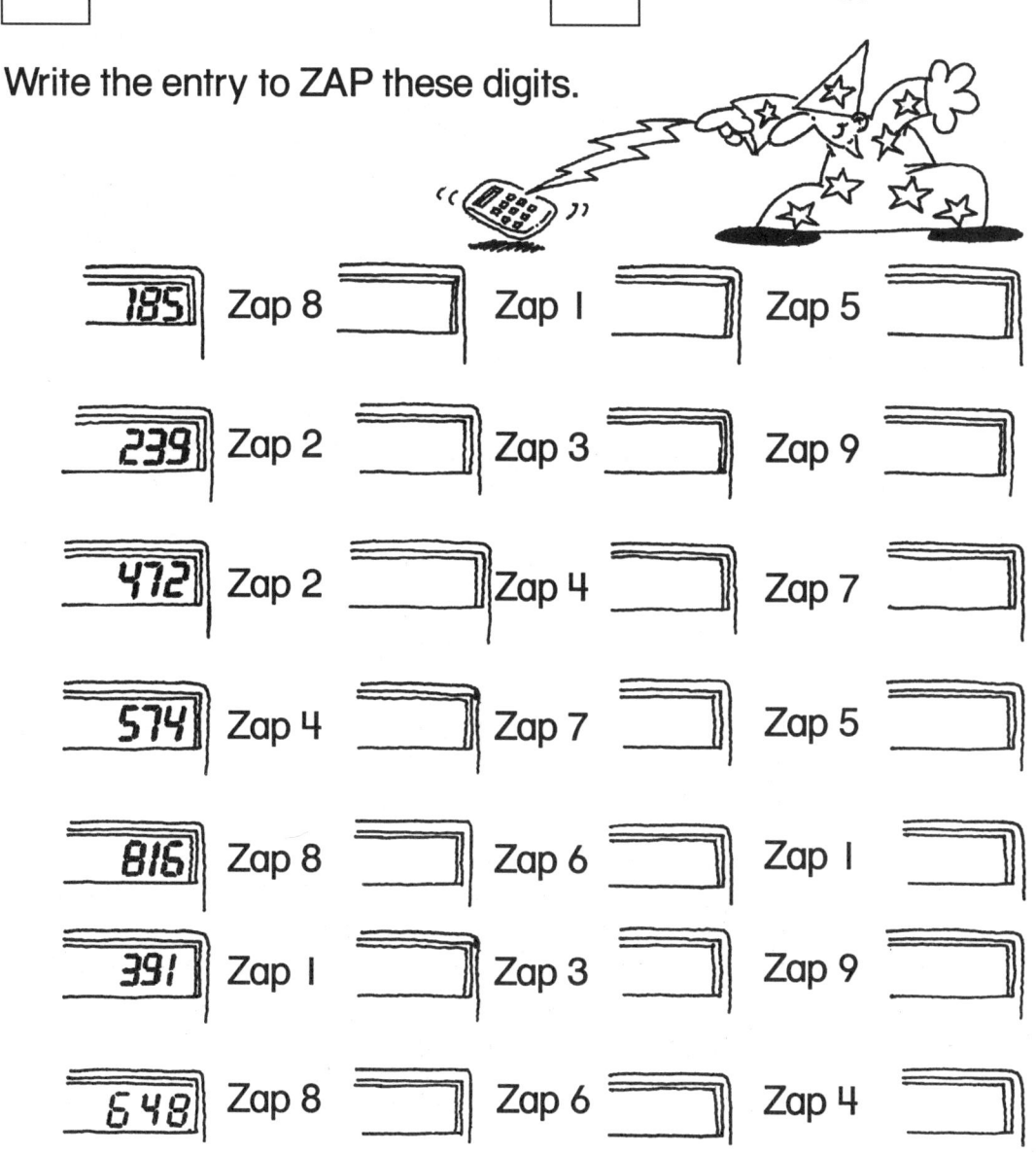

648 Zap 8 ____ Zap 6 ____ Zap 4 ____

14. Say Ninety-Nine

Start with a 3-digit number *693*

Reverse the digits. *396*

Subtract the small number from the large number. *693 − 396*

Difference *297*

Do the same again. *792 − 297*

Difference *495*

Do the same again. *594 − 495*

Difference *99*

Try the same with other 3-digit numbers.

Start with *723*   Start with *852*   Choose your own starting number.

15. Unlucky Code

52	65	78	91	104	117	130	143	156	169	182	195	208
A	E	K	M	H	Y	T	C	Q	N	W	P	U

221	234	247	260	273	286	299	312	325	338	351	364	377
X	B	I	L	F	D	G	J	O	S	V	R	Z

Multiply each number by 13.
Use your answers to crack the code.

21　28　19　22　4　9　　10　8　5

10　8　19　28　10　5　5　13　10　8

22　25　　13　25　10　　14　4　20　6

16　13　22　5　28　　20　4　22　22　5　28　26

16. Table Teaser

A square and a rectangle have been drawn on the table square.
Multiply the numbers in the opposite corners together.

The square:

4 × 16 = ☐   8 × 8 = ☐

The rectangle:

18 × 42 = ☐   21 × 36 = ☐

1	2	3	4	5	6	7	8	9	10	11	12
2	4	6	8	10	12	14	16	18	20	22	24
3	6	9	12	15	18	21	24	27	30	33	36
4	8	12	16	20	24	28	32	36	40	44	48
5	10	15	20	25	30	35	40	45	50	55	60
6	12	18	24	30	36	42	48	54	60	66	72
7	14	21	28	35	42	49	56	63	70	77	84
8	16	24	32	40	48	56	64	72	80	88	96
9	18	27	36	45	54	63	72	81	90	99	108
10	20	30	40	50	60	70	80	90	100	110	120
11	22	33	44	55	66	77	88	99	110	121	132
12	24	36	48	60	72	84	96	108	120	132	144

What do you notice?
Draw 6 more squares and rectangles on the table square.
Multiply the corner numbers.
What do you notice?

17. Island Journey

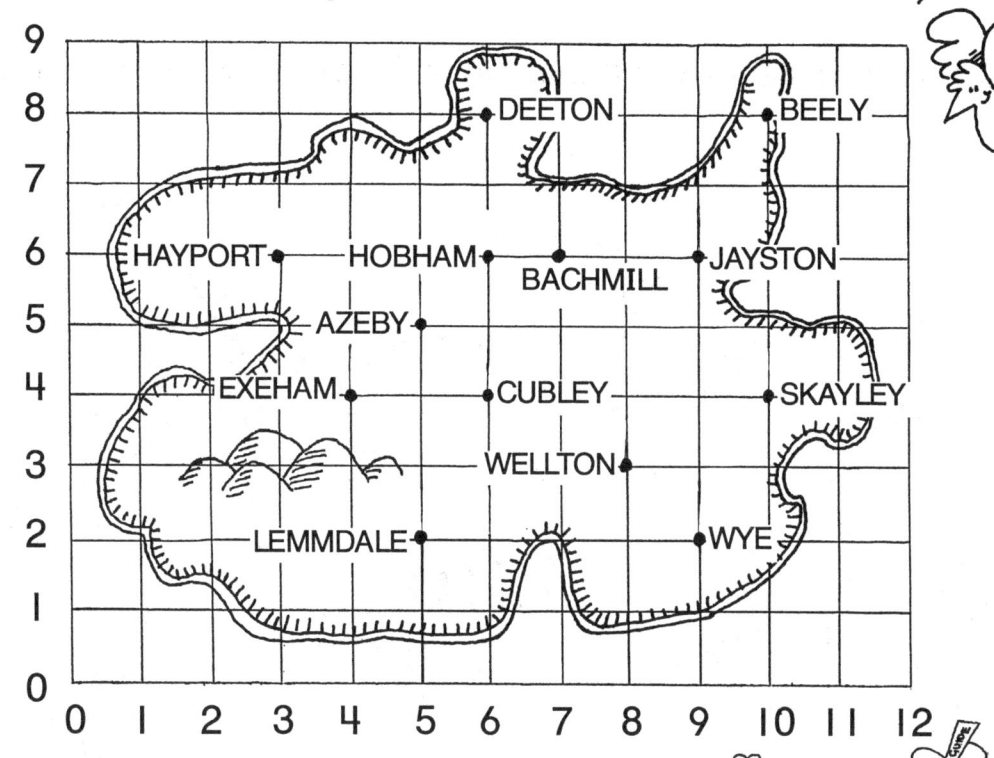

684 ÷ 19 = 36
Look at the answer.
On the map go 3 along then 6 up.
You will find the town of Hayport.
Meg visited this town.
Find the other towns Meg visited.

544 ÷ 8 _____   912 ÷ 12 _____
864 ÷ 9 _____   581 ÷ 7 _____
828 ÷ 9 _____   676 ÷ 13 _____
896 ÷ 14 _____   792 ÷ 18 _____
880 ÷ 16 _____   858 ÷ 13 _____

She did not visit two towns.
Which two were they?   _____   _____

18. Find the Launcher

Connect each rocket to its launcher to make the total on the moon.

19. Turn and Turn Again

Write any three digit number.
The first digit must be at
least 2 bigger than the last.

Reverse the number.

Subtract the numbers.

Reverse the answer.

Add the last two rows of numbers.

7	4	2
2	4	7
4	9	5
5	9	4
1089

Try with some three digit numbers of your own:

What do you notice?

20. The Broken Key

The calculator has a broken key.
The 9 key is broken.
The calculator was still used to work out 97 + 85.
This is how it was done:

85 + 97

$\boxed{85}\ \boxed{+}\ \boxed{100}\ \boxed{-}\ \boxed{3}\ \boxed{=}\ \boxed{182}$

You will notice that the 97 has been rounded up to 100 to avoid using the 9 key.

Do these without using your 9 key.

138 + 192
199 + 178
209 + 193
94 + 196
517 − 189
619 − 84
390 − 139
209 − 95

21. Crack the Code

Find the answer to the coded question.
Here is the key to the code.

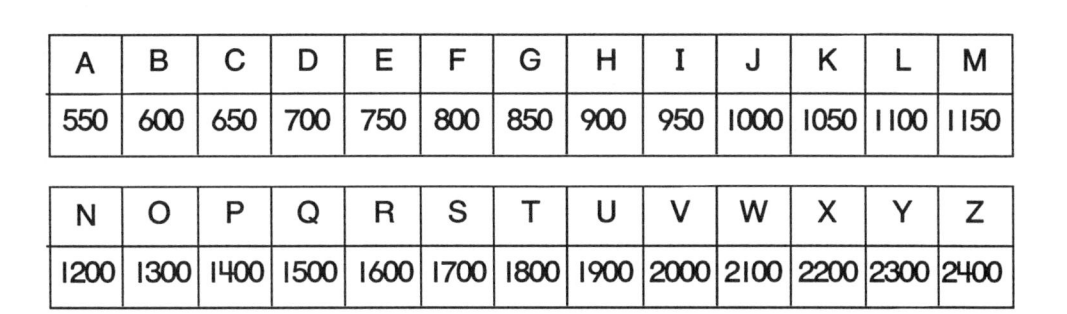

A	B	C	D	E	F	G	H	I	J	K	L	M
550	600	650	700	750	800	850	900	950	1000	1050	1100	1150

N	O	P	Q	R	S	T	U	V	W	X	Y	Z
1200	1300	1400	1500	1600	1700	1800	1900	2000	2100	2200	2300	2400

35 × 60	45 × 20	50 × 11	45 × 40
W	H	A	T

174 + 776	942 + 758
I	S

45 × 40	90 × 10	30 × 25
T	H	E

60 × 20	50 × 15	22 × 100	36 × 50
N	E	X	T

1499 + 201	650 + 850	911 + 989	321 + 229	950 + 650	430 + 320
S	Q	U	A	R	E

591 + 609	951 + 949	557 + 593	330 + 270	99 + 651	773 + 827
N	U	M	B	E	R

11 × 50	40 × 20	60 × 30	75 × 10	40 × 40
A	F	T	E	R

80 × 15	19 × 50	40 × 30	375 × 2	?
N	I	N	E	

Answer: 16

22. Times and Times Again

Each of these answers has been made by multiplying three consecutive numbers. Can you find them?

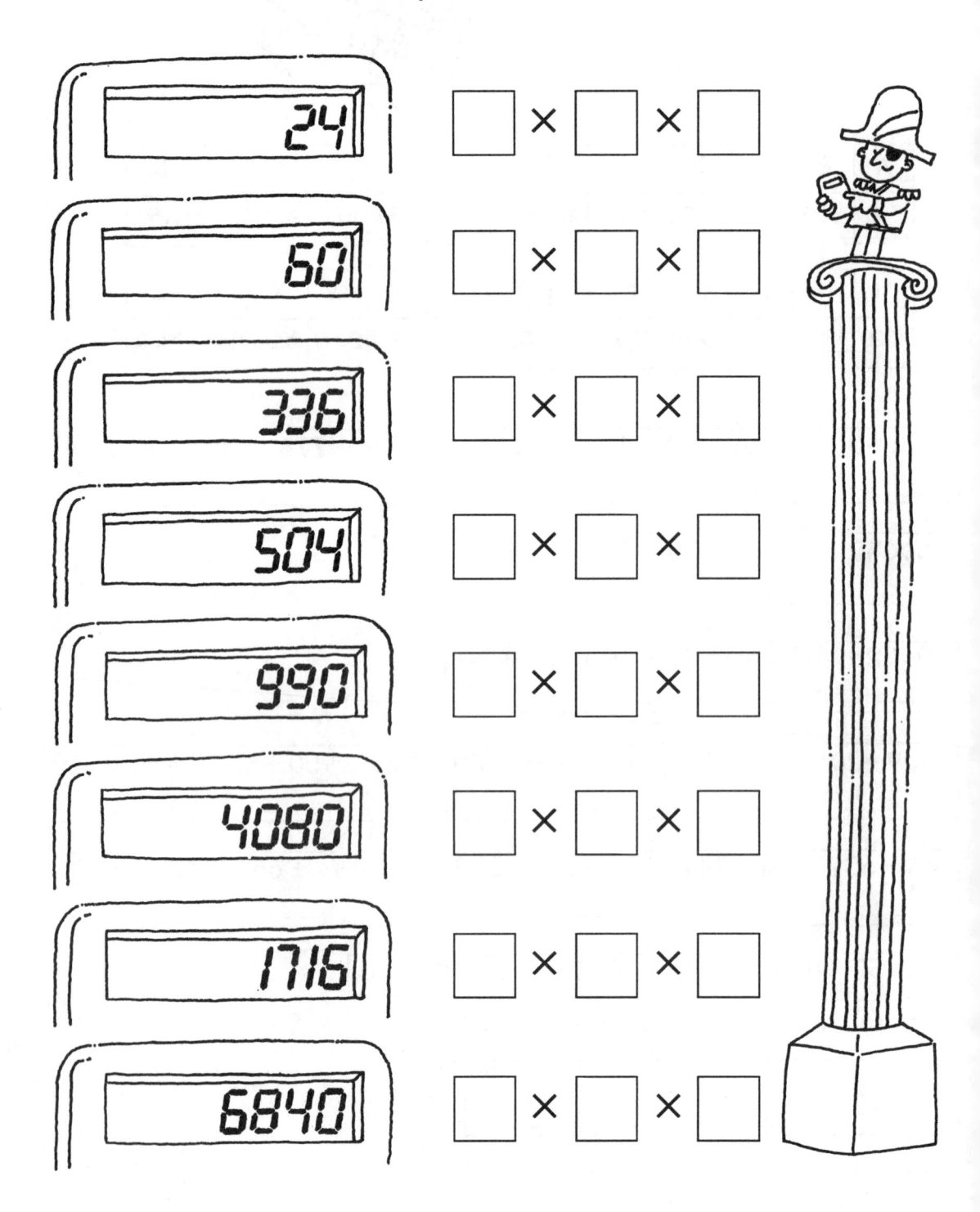

24 = ☐ × ☐ × ☐

60 = ☐ × ☐ × ☐

336 = ☐ × ☐ × ☐

504 = ☐ × ☐ × ☐

990 = ☐ × ☐ × ☐

4080 = ☐ × ☐ × ☐

1716 = ☐ × ☐ × ☐

6840 = ☐ × ☐ × ☐

23. Number Words on Display

Across
(number clues)   (word clues)

2 Double 2855   Used in painting
6 (847 × 5) + (700 × 5) Opposite of 'buy'
8 (5000 − 241) × 4 × 3   Water does this when heated
9 154 × 2 × 10   A musical instrument
10 $\frac{2}{3}$ of 771   Belongs to him
11 $\frac{705}{1000}$ On your own

Down

1 2204 ÷ 2 × 7   You can climb this
3 (9 × 615) + 2   Opposite of 'more'
4 1616 halved   A boy's name
5 (99 + 4) × 6   Large
7 (847 + 820) × 3 × 7   Not tight
10 1000 − 196   Found in an old fireplace

24. Treasure Trail

Which treasure will you find?
Look for the answers to each multiplication in the DIRECTIONS BOX. This will tell you which direction to move.
Move to the next junction.
Keep going until you reach the treasure.

SAPPHIRES

69 × 87
74 × 87
58 × 48
86 × 76
49 × 86
96 × 58
86 × 65
43 × 76
57 × 69
87 × 86
89 × 47
87 × 65

DIAMONDS

START
N

GOLD

RUBIES

SILVER

DIRECTIONS BOX

Move N	Move S	Move E	Move W
4183	6536	5655	3933
5568	3268	5590	
	6003	6438	
	4214		
	7482		

Which treasure did you find?

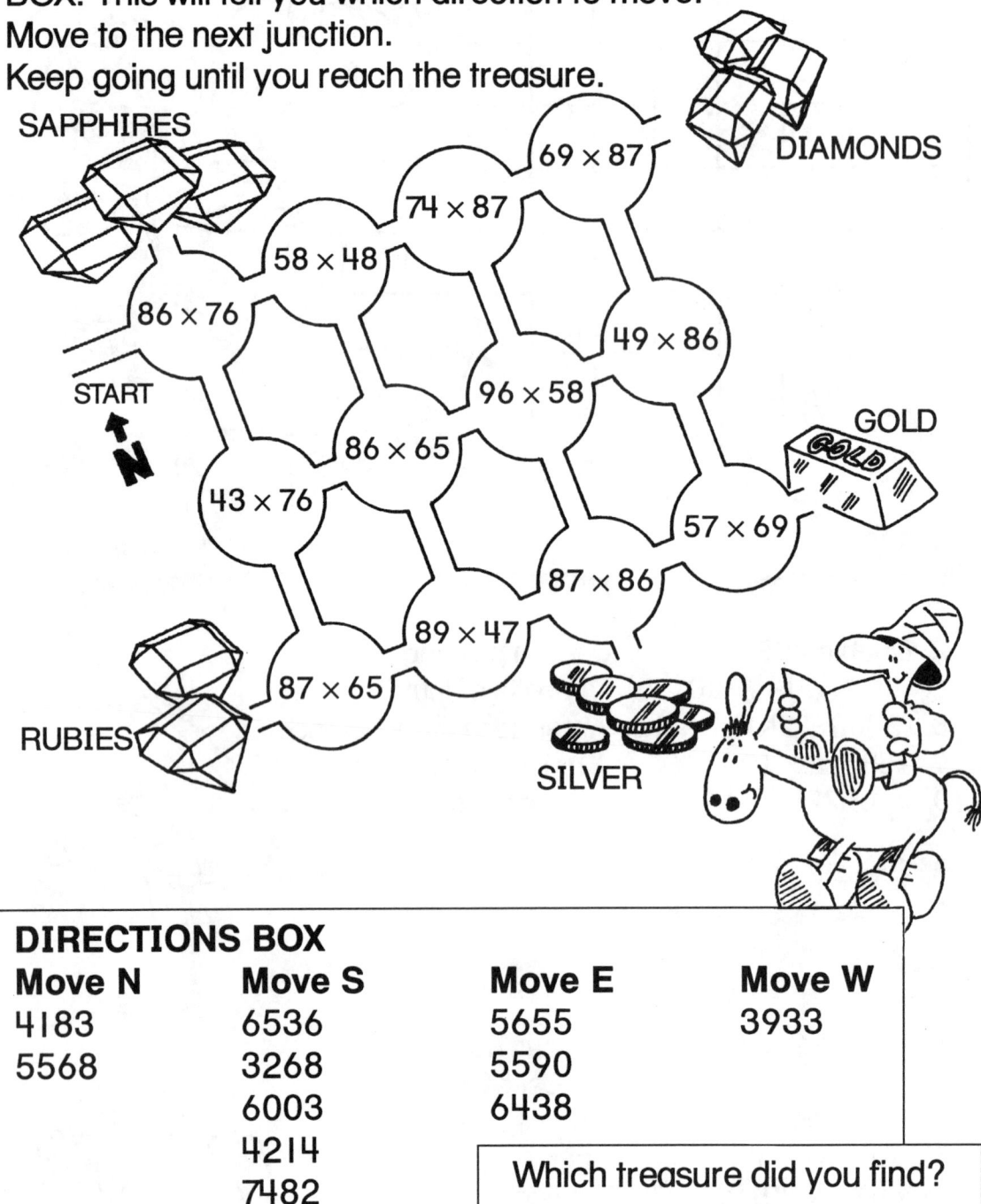

25. Find the Twin

Write the answer on each elephant.
Join the pairs that give the same answer.

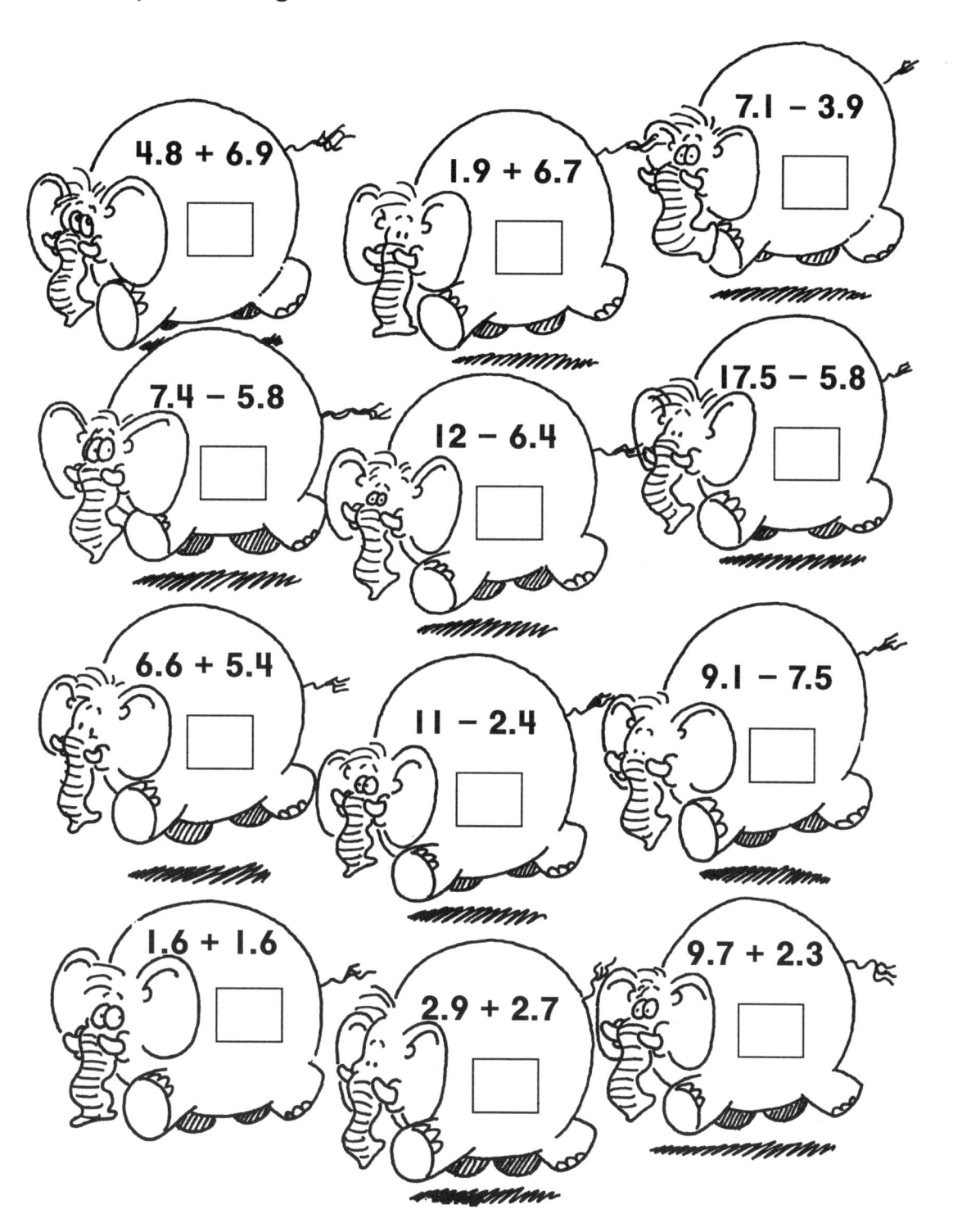

4.8 + 6.9

1.9 + 6.7

7.1 − 3.9

7.4 − 5.8

12 − 6.4

17.5 − 5.8

6.6 + 5.4

11 − 2.4

9.1 − 7.5

1.6 + 1.6

2.9 + 2.7

9.7 + 2.3

26. Deci-Aliens Landing

You can stop the deci-aliens if their total is 1. Display each number in turn on your calculator. Input the addition you think will make it 1. If the display shows 1, then cross out the deci-alien. It is destroyed. If not try another input.

0.6 +
0.8 +
0.3 +
0.5 +
0.7 +
0.2 +
0.4 +
0.94 +
0.61 +
0.16 +
0.33 +
0.47 +
0.82 +
0.66 +
0.79 +
0.11 +
0.59 +
0.25 +
0.76 +
0.99 +
0.78 +
0.42 +
0.38 +
0.74 +
0.81 +

27. Lift Off

Fill in the missing numbers to launch the spaceship.
You can find the answers by working backwards.

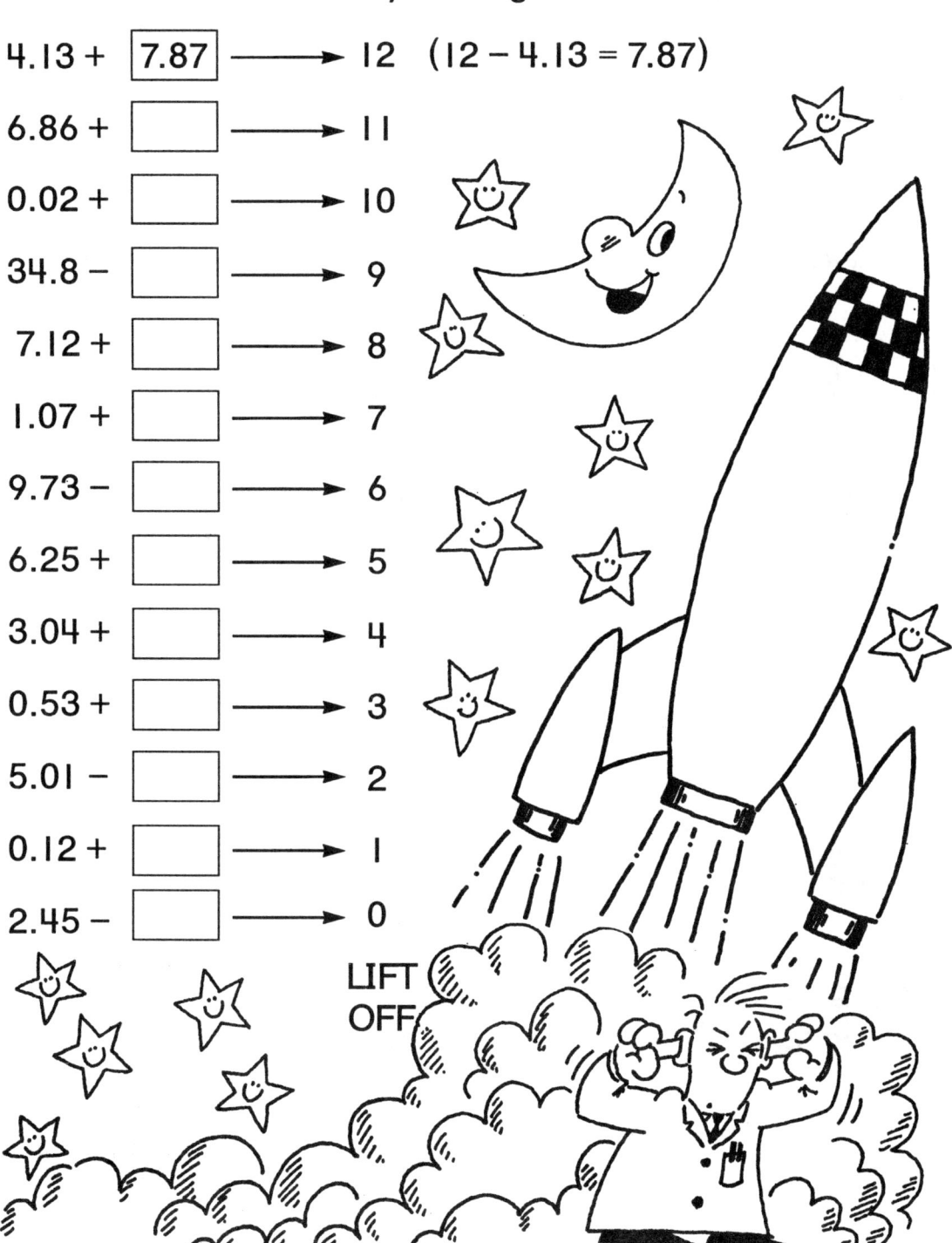

4.13 + [7.87] → 12   (12 − 4.13 = 7.87)
6.86 + [ ] → 11
0.02 + [ ] → 10
34.8 − [ ] → 9
7.12 + [ ] → 8
1.07 + [ ] → 7
9.73 − [ ] → 6
6.25 + [ ] → 5
3.04 + [ ] → 4
0.53 + [ ] → 3
5.01 − [ ] → 2
0.12 + [ ] → 1
2.45 − [ ] → 0

LIFT OFF

28. Patterns Without Limits

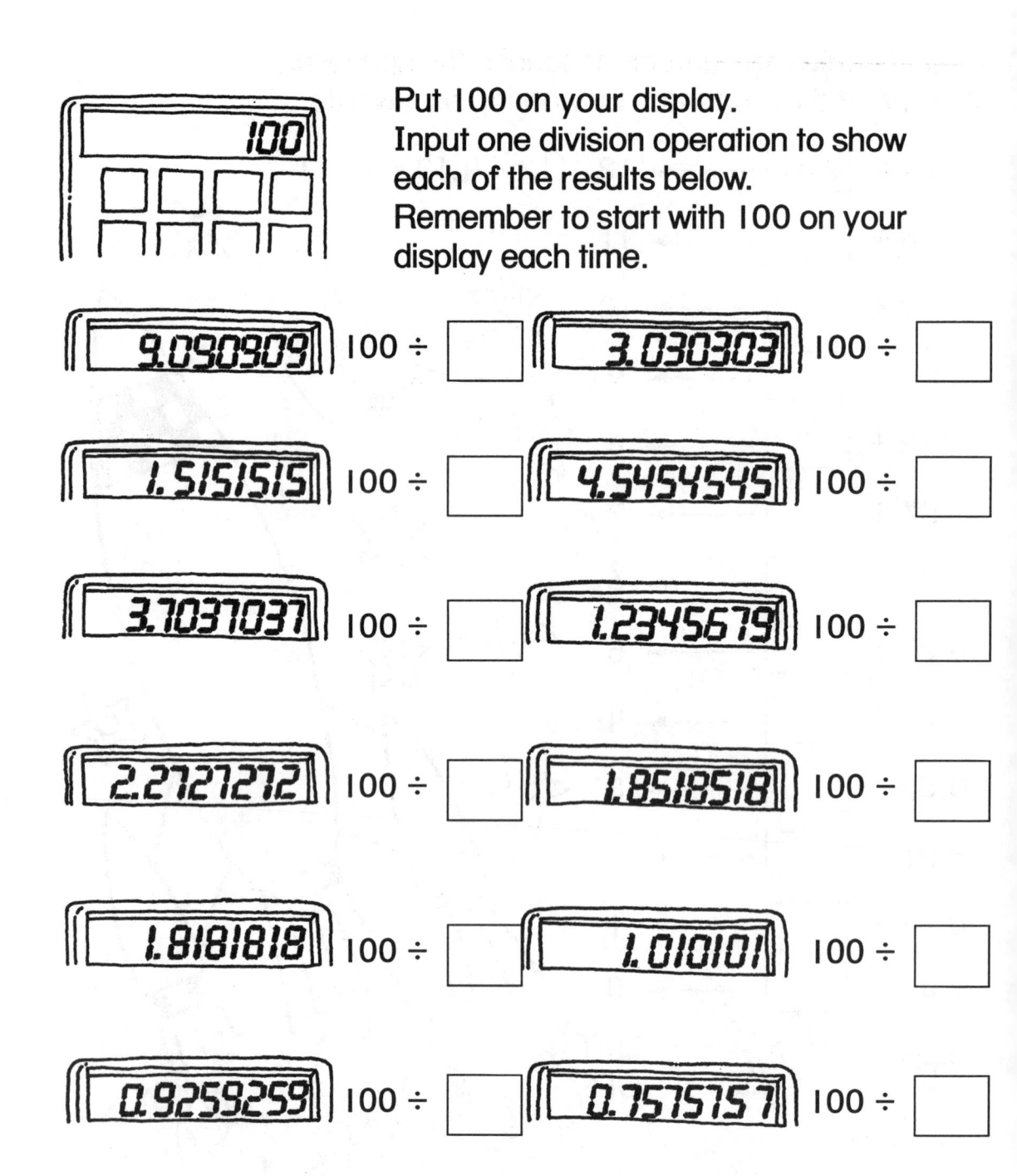

Put 100 on your display.
Input one division operation to show each of the results below.
Remember to start with 100 on your display each time.

9.090909	100 ÷ ☐	3.030303	100 ÷ ☐
1.515151	100 ÷ ☐	4.545454	100 ÷ ☐
3.7037037	100 ÷ ☐	1.2345679	100 ÷ ☐
2.2727272	100 ÷ ☐	1.8518518	100 ÷ ☐
1.8181818	100 ÷ ☐	1.010101	100 ÷ ☐
0.9259259	100 ÷ ☐	0.7575757	100 ÷ ☐

Answers

1. **Butterflies**
   They catch seven butterflies.

2. **Target**

9 = 3 + 3 + 3	14 = 5 + 3 + 3 + 3
13 = 5 + 5 + 3	18 = 5 + 5 + 5 + 3
1 = 3 + 3 − 5	17 = 5 + 5 + 5 + 5 − 3
4 = 3 + 3 + 3 − 5	11 = 5 + 3 + 3

1 = 7 − 2 − 2 − 2	13 = 7 + 2 + 2 + 2
3 = 7 − 2 − 2	17 = 7 + 7 + 7 − 2 − 2
11 = 7 + 2 + 2	19 = 7 + 7 + 7 − 2
12 = 7 + 7 − 2	21 = 7 + 7 + 7

3. **Four In a Line**
   A game.

4. **Number Magic**
   All your answers should come to 23.

5. **Just Two**
   2 = 6 + 6 − 5 − 5
   3 = 5 + 5 + 5 − 6 − 6
   4 = 5 + 5 − 6
   5 = 5 + 6 − 6
   6 = 6 + 5 − 5
   7 = 6 + 6 − 5
   8 = 6 + 6 + 6 − 5 − 5
   9 = 5 + 5 + 5 − 6
   10 = 5 + 5

6. **Bats in the Belfry**
   There are 6 bats with an EVEN number.

7. **Making Centuries**
   +53 +37 +79 +66 +22 +48 +85 +11

8. **Taking Centuries**
   −22 −51 −83 −68 −59 −37 −45 −74

9. **Find the Shape**
   The shape is a robot.

10. **Wheel Code**
    The box contains: A SMALL BLACK AND WHITE KITTEN.

11. **Count Down**

10 = 9 + 8 − 7	9 = 5 × 3 − 6
8 = 6 × 4 ÷ 3	7 = 4 + 8 − 5
6 = 7 × 2 − 8	5 = 9 ÷ 3 + 2
4 = 8 × 3 ÷ 6	3 = 5 − 4 × 3
2 = 8 + 6 ÷ 7	1 = 6 ÷ 2 − 2
0 = 9 ÷ 3 − 3	

12. **Number Words On Display**
    The shop keeper SELLS.

ACROSS	DOWN
1. HIS	2. SHELL
3. HOLE	4. EGGS
5. ILL	6. LOG
7. OIL	
8. HOG	
9. LEGS	

13. **Zap the Digit**

185 − 80	105 − 100	5 − 5	0
239 − 200	39 − 30	9 − 9	0
472 − 2	470 − 400	70 − 70	0
574 − 4	570 − 70	500 − 500	0
816 − 800	16 − 6	10 − 10	0
391 − 1	390 − 300	90 − 90	0
648 − 8	640 − 600	40 − 40	0

14. **Say Ninety-Nine**
    You will always end up with 99.

15. **Unlucky Code**
    The coded message is: FRIDAY THE THIRTEENTH.
    DO NOT WALK UNDER LADDERS.

16. **Table Teasers**
    When you multiply corner numbers
    you get the same answer.

17. **Island Journey**
    The towns not visited are BEELY and SKAYLEY.

18. **Find the Launcher**

103 + 123	79 + 147
92 + 134	93 + 133
36 + 190	87 + 139
112 + 114	75 + 151
	84 + 142

19. **Turn and Turn Again**
    You should always get the answer 1089.

20. **The Broken Key**
    There are several ways of getting the answers
    without using the 9 key. Here is one example of each.

138 + 192	=	138 + 202 − 10	=	330
199 + 178	=	200 + 177	=	377
209 + 193	=	210 + 203 − 11	=	402
94 + 196	=	84 + 206	=	290
517 − 189	=	517 − 188 − 1	=	328
619 − 84	=	620 − 85	=	535
390 − 139	=	380 − 128 − 1	=	251
209 − 95	=	210 − 106 + 10	=	114

21. Crack the Code
    What is the next square number after nine?
    The answer is sixteen.

22. Times and Times Again
    $24 = 2 \times 3 \times 4$ $60 = 3 \times 4 \times 5$
    $336 = 6 \times 7 \times 8$ $504 = 7 \times 8 \times 9$
    $990 = 9 \times 10 \times 11$ $4080 = 15 \times 16 \times 17$
    $1716 = 11 \times 12 \times 13$ $6840 = 18 \times 19 \times 20$

23. Number Words On Display
    ACROSS   DOWN
    2. OILS   1. HILL
    6. SELL   2. LESS
    8. BOILS   4. BOB
    9. OBOE   5. BIG
    10. HIS   7. LOOSE
    11. SOLO   10. HOB

24. Treasure Trail
    You should find the treasure; SILVER

25. Find the Twin
    $1.9 + 6.7 = 8.6$ $7.1 - 3.9 = 3.2$
    $11 - 2.4 = 8.6$ $1.6 + 1.6 = 3.2$

    $7.4 - 5.8 = 1.6$ $12 - 6.4 = 5.6$
    $9.1 - 7.5 = 1.6$ $2.9 + 2.7 = 5.6$

    $6.6 + 5.4 = 12$
    $9.7 + 2.3 = 12$

26. Deci-Aliens Landing
    $0.6 + 0.4$ $0.8 + 0.2$ $0.3 + 0.7$ $0.5 + 0.5$
    $0.7 + 0.3$ $0.2 + 0.8$ $0.4 + 0.6$
    $0.94 + 0.06$ $0.61 + 0.39$ $0.16 + 0.84$ $0.33 + 0.67$
    $0.47 + 0.53$ $0.82 + 0.18$ $0.66 + 0.34$
    $0.79 + 0.21$ $0.11 + 0.89$ $0.59 + 0.41$ $0.25 + 0.75$
    $0.76 + 0.24$ $0.99 + 0.01$ $0.78 + 0.22$
    $0.42 + 0.58$ $0.38 + 0.62$ $0.74 + 0.26$ $0.81 + 0.19$

27. Lift Off
    $6.86 + 4.14 \rightarrow 11$ $6.25 - 1.25 \rightarrow 5$
    $0.02 + 9.98 \rightarrow 10$ $3.04 + 0.96 \rightarrow 4$
    $34.8 + 25.8 \rightarrow 9$ $0.53 + 2.47 \rightarrow 3$
    $7.12 + 0.88 \rightarrow 8$ $5.01 - 3.01 \rightarrow 2$
    $1.07 + 5.93 \rightarrow 7$ $0.12 + 0.88 \rightarrow 1$
    $9.73 - 3.73 \rightarrow 6$ $2.45 - 2.45 \rightarrow 0$

28. Patterns Without Limits
    $100 \div 11$ $100 \div 33$
    $100 \div 66$ $100 \div 22$
    $100 \div 27$ $100 \div 81$
    $100 \div 44$ $100 \div 54$
    $100 \div 55$ $100 \div 99$
    $100 \div 108$ $100 \div 132$